Collins

Primary Social Studies for Antigua and Barbuda

WORKBOOK
GRADE 2

T0320910

Anthea S Thomas

William Collins' dream of knowledge for all began with the publication of his first book in 1819.
A self-educated mill worker, he not only enriched millions of lives, but also founded a flourishing publishing house. Today, staying true to this spirit, Collins books are packed with inspiration, innovation and practical expertise. They place you at the centre of a world of possibility and give you exactly what you need to explore it.

Collins. Freedom to teach.

Published by Collins
An imprint of HarperCollins*Publishers*
The News Building
1 London Bridge Street
London SE1 9GF

HarperCollins*Publishers*
Macken House, 39/40 Mayor Street Upper,
Dublin 1, D01 C9W8, Ireland

Browse the complete Collins Caribbean catalogue at
www.collins.co.uk/caribbeanschools

10 9 8 7 6 5

ISBN 978-0-00-840283-9

British Library Cataloguing-in-Publication Data
A catalogue record for this publication is available from the British Library.

Author: Anthea S. Thomas
Publisher: Elaine Higgleton
In-house senior editor: Julianna Dunn
Development & copy editor: Sue Chapple
Proof reader & answer checker: Mitch Fitton
Cover designers: Kevin Robbins and Gordon MacGilp
Cover image: Wectors/Shutterstock
Typesetter: QBS
Illustrators: Danielle Boodoo-Fortuné & QBS
Production controller: Lyndsey Rogers
Printed and Bound in the UK by Ashford Colour Press Ltd

Acknowledgements

The publishers wish to thank the following for permission to reproduce photographs. Every effort has been made to trace copyright holders and to obtain their permission for the use of copyright materials. The publishers will gladly receive any information enabling them to rectify any error or omission at the first opportunity.
(t = top, c = centre, b = bottom, l = left, r = right)

p20a: Clive Chilvers/SS, p20b: sansak/SS, p20c: ZoranKrstic/SS, p20d: SusaZoom/SS, p23t: Shutterstock, p23b: Shutterstock, p25a: Atlaspix/SS, p25b: Alex Staroseltsev/SS, p26c: Pixcellentprintsltd/SS, p26d: Isabelle Kuehn/SS, p26e: Don Mammoser/SS, p26f: Robert Fried / Alamy Stock Photo, p26g: Fanfo/SS, p26h: Paul B. Moore/SS, p27i: photowind/SS, p27j: Amy Katherine Dragoo / Alamy Stock Photo, p28: George Brice / Alamy Stock Photo, p29a: EQRoy/SS, p29b: Sarah Cheriton-Jones/SS, p29c: PlusONE/SS, p29d: Donianna Forde/SS, p30: George Brice / Alamy Stock Photo, p32l: Lux Blue/SS, p32r: byvalet/SS, p38 top row left-right: Ste studio/SS, Maike Hildebrandt/SS, Ksenya Savva/SS, simpleicon/SS, veronchick_84/SS, p38 bottom row left-right: liluydesign/SS, vectorchef/SS, Bowrann/SS, LWY Partnership/SS, p40 top row left - right: Elsham/SS, Pavel K/SS, Icon Craft Studio/SS, p40 bottom row left-right: Janis Abolins/SS, Rvector/SS, HN Works/SS, p47 top left: sirtravelalot/SS, p47 top right: Ze.Elias65/SS, p47 middle left: shipfactory/SS, p47 middle right: Phonlamai Photo/SS, p47 bottom left: Asier Romero/SS, p47 bottom right: Inhabitant/SS, p53a: Andre Adams/SS, p53b: Kolonko/SS, p53c: yavi/SS, p53d: KlaraDo/SS, p53e: Anna Frajtova/SS, p53f: Biscotto Design/SS, p57: GraphicsRF/SS, p59a: Drew McArthur/SS, p59b: Olha Rohulya/SS, p59c: chrisontour84/SS, p59d: Gabriele Maltinti/SS.

Contents

1 Individuals in groups

Student's Book pages 4–12

1 Draw a picture of yourself in the box below. Write three sentences that describe you.

a _____

_____

b _____

_____

c _____

_____

2 Draw a simple map of where you live in the box. Make sure you include roads and trees. Write the name of your community below.

3 Use words from the box to fill in the blank spaces in the sentences.

> community   family   in common   neighbourhood
>
> small   single

a An individual is a _____ person.

b A group is a set of people who have something _____.

c A _____ is an example of a group.

d Families can be large or _____.

e Families living close together make up a _____.

f Several neighbourhoods make up a _____.

4 Use words from the box to fill in the blank spaces in the sentences.

> **Arawaks** **food** **Amerindians** **Waladli**
>
> **Caribs** **South America**

a Long, long ago, people came from _____ to settle
in Antigua.

b They were known as the _____.

c There were two groups, the _____ and the

_____.

d They came in search of _____.

e The Carib name for Antigua was _____.

5 Write five things the Amerindians did in order to survive.

_____

_____

_____

_____

_____

_____

_____

6 Fill in the blanks in this sentence

Two groups of people who came after the Amerindians are the

_____ and the _____ .

7 Who am I?

Use words from the box to answer the questions.

> **A European**   **An Amerindian**   **Sugarcane**
>
> **A Chinese person**   **A slave**

a I am one of the first group of people to live in Antigua and Barbuda.

Who am I ? _____

b I came from West Africa to work on the sugar plantation.

Who am I ? _____

c I am grown on a sugar plantation.

What am I ? _____

d I came as an indentured worker.

Who am I ? _____

8 Answer these questions.

a People who are in the same ethnic group have lots of things in common. Write four things they have in common.

_____

_____

_____

_____

b What country were you born in?

_____

c What is your nationality?

_____

9 Make a list of 10 different nationalities and ethnic groups living in Antigua and Barbuda.

_____

_____

_____

_____

_____

_____

_____

_____

_____

_____

10 Are these statements True or False? Write T or F after each one.

a People in a community are all the same age. ☐

b People living in a community do different jobs. ☐

c People living in a community all have the same religious beliefs. ☐

d People living in a community share and care for each other. ☐

11 On this map of Antigua, write in the names of the six parishes. Write the names of two towns or villages found in each parish.

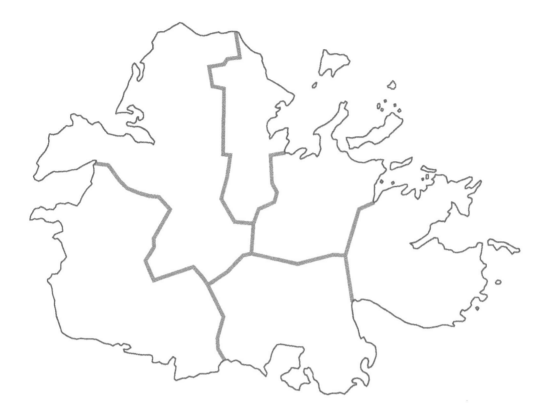

12 Find these words in the puzzle.

AMERINDIANS

COMMUNITY

ETHNIC

GROUP

INDIVIDUAL

LIFESTYLE

NATIONALITY

PARISH

RELIGION

SETTLE

T	Y	X	L	P	R	C	X	H	A	Y	G	Q	A	J
M	N	T	R	I	I	G	S	F	T	I	R	M	M	L
C	L	W	I	N	F	I	B	I	D	Z	O	L	E	W
F	L	O	H	N	R	E	L	L	D	G	U	Q	R	A
F	S	T	P	A	U	A	S	J	R	Z	P	R	I	T
D	E	V	P	M	N	M	T	T	Z	X	J	E	N	V
V	S	M	H	O	C	A	M	J	Y	L	Q	L	D	S
O	K	P	I	T	E	M	N	O	P	L	X	I	I	S
Z	Y	T	S	E	T	T	L	E	C	U	E	G	A	N
F	A	L	W	V	A	A	L	I	A	D	G	I	N	V
N	A	M	E	I	Y	X	W	S	M	K	F	O	S	G
M	T	D	Y	L	Y	Q	L	B	D	I	Y	N	G	V
T	M	K	F	J	O	T	V	P	R	D	N	D	P	Z
K	N	M	K	L	B	J	R	Z	R	B	A	Q	N	C
I	N	D	I	V	I	D	U	A	L	O	P	J	W	K

2 Living in Antigua and Barbuda

Student's Book pages 13–23

1 Use words from the box to fill in the blank spaces in the sentences.

single-parent   family   extended   nuclear

a   A _____ is a group of people living together and who are related to each other by blood or adoption.

b   A family with a mother and father, and with a child or children is a

_____ family.

c   A family with a mother and children, or a father and children, is a

_____ family.

d   A family with grandparents, parents, children, and maybe other relatives

too, is an _____ family.

2 Draw a picture of your family. Include all the people you live with. Write a sentence below about each member of your family.

3 A family tree shows the relationship between members of a family. Look at this family tree, then fill in the blanks in the sentences.

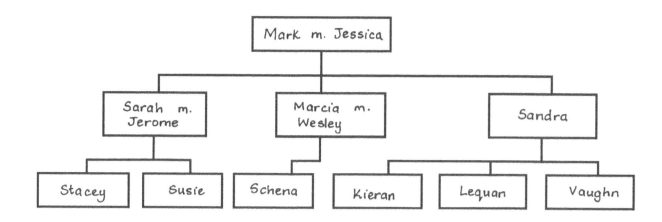

Mark m. Jessica

Sarah m. Jerome

Marcia m. Wesley

Sandra

Stacey

Susie

Schena

Kieran

Lequan

Vaughn

a Kieran's grandmother's name is _____ .

b Sarah is Kieran's _____ .

c Kieran's mother is Sarah's _____ .

d Stacey and Susie are two of Kieran's _____ .

e Kieran's brothers are _____ and _____ .

4 Draw your own family tree in the box.

5 Read about Stacey and her family, then answer the questions.

> Stacey is seven years old. Her mother had a baby boy last month. Her big brother Mark, who is 20, got married and went to live in another village with his wife. Stacey's grandfather got the flu recently, and died.

a Did Stacey's family change? _____

b What were the changes? _____

_____

_____

_____

_____

_____

c How do you think Stacey felt when she got a new baby brother?

_____

_____

d How do you think she felt when her brother got married?

_____

_____

e How do you think she felt when her grandfather died?

_____

_____

6 What are some of the things that your family celebrate? Draw a picture of one of them in the box below.

_____

_____

_____

_____

_____

_____

7 What are some of the celebrations that take place in your community? Draw a picture of one of them in the box below.

_____

_____

_____

_____

_____

_____

_____

8 Write the name of the celebration shown in each picture.

a _____

b _____

c _____

d _____

9 Use words from the box to fill in the blank spaces in the sentences.

custom	grandparents	church	tradition
culture	storytelling	culture	school

a The way we live is called our _____.

b We can learn a lot about our _____ from our

_____.

c When culture is passed on from one generation to the next it is called

_____.

d _____ can be used to pass on a tradition.

e The way you usually do something is called a _____.

f We can also learn about culture and heritage from _____

and _____.

10 Fill in the table to show some differences between life for children long ago and life for children today.

How children lived long ago	How children live today

11 Help Shania find her way through the maze back to her family.

12 Find these words in the puzzle.

CELEBRATIONS

CUSTOMS

DIALECT

EMOTIONS

FAMILY

FEELINGS

FESTIVAL

FOLKLORE

HERITAGE

HYGIENE

PRAY

TRADITIONS

C	Q	S	O	E	N	S	I	J	J	F	P	M	F	U
D	E	F	N	G	G	V	A	V	S	S	O	O	F	E
I	Q	L	B	O	R	A	G	I	C	P	L	P	E	M
A	J	C	E	H	I	K	T	G	M	K	F	S	E	O
L	W	T	T	B	G	T	J	I	L	N	X	M	L	T
E	C	G	T	U	R	R	I	O	R	C	Q	O	I	I
C	A	T	Y	H	W	A	R	D	Y	E	H	T	N	O
T	D	O	S	Y	Z	E	T	T	A	Y	H	S	G	N
F	E	S	T	I	V	A	L	I	G	R	Y	U	S	S
G	Z	D	W	O	L	R	F	I	O	A	T	C	Q	X
G	L	L	H	G	X	T	E	A	R	N	K	T	A	U
O	E	O	B	L	O	N	N	P	M	H	S	P	V	B
V	N	N	P	K	E	R	U	Z	C	I	G	G	G	S
M	P	I	G	Z	G	E	O	O	C	D	L	P	D	S
K	K	X	W	Z	Y	U	X	R	N	H	X	Y	L	C

3 What does it mean to be Antiguan and Barbudan?

Student's Book pages 24–36

1 Use words from the box to fill in the blank spaces in the sentences.

> second   culture   symbols   values   identify
>
> Sir Novelle Richards   history

a Each country has national _____ that help to

    _____ that country.

b Symbols are important because they show the _____,

    _____ and _____ we have as a country.

c The national anthem was written by _____.

d The national motto is in the _____ verse of the national anthem.

2 These are all national symbols of Antigua and Barbuda. Write the name of each one below the picture.

EACH ENDEAVOURING ALL ACHIEVING

a _____   b _____

c _____

d _____

e _____

f _____

g _____

h _____

i _____   j _____

3 Colour in the national flag of Antigua and Barbuda. Write what each colour means below.

a Gold = _____

b Red = _____

c Black = _____

d Blue = _____

e Yellow, blue and white = _____

Sir Vere Cornwall Bird

Dame Nellie Robinson

Sir Isaac Vivian Richards

Prince Klass

5 Are these statements True or False? Write T or F after each one.

a We should destroy our national symbols.

b We should stand to attention when the national anthem
is being played.

c National symbols are not important.

d National heroes are national symbols.

6 Write the names of the historical sites shown in the pictures.

a _____

b _____

c _____

d _____

7 Read the text and then answer the questions.

Sir Viv Richards is one of our living national heroes. He is a famous cricketer. Some say he was the best batsman ever. He travelled around the world and made Antigua and Barbuda famous. He played in countries such as England and India.

a What is the name of the national hero shown in the picture?

_____

b What sport did he play? _____

c Name one country that he played in. _____

8 Think of any historical sites in or near your local community.

    a Name two of them.

    _____

    _____

    b Try to find a picture of them and stick them below.

9 Look at these two buildings. Write two ways in which they are the same and two ways in which they are different.

_____

_____

_____

_____

_____

_____

10 How have buildings in your community changed over the years? Think about what the buildings look like and what they are used for.

_____

_____

_____

_____

_____

_____

11 Use words from the box to fill in the blank spaces in the sentences.

| East | West | North | South |

a Your home is _____ of your school.

b The ball field is _____ of your home.

c The principal's office is _____ of your classroom.

d Your church is _____ of your home.

12 Look at the map of part of the Caribbean and answer the questions. Each answer is a point of the compass.

a Antigua is _____ of Barbuda.

b Dominica is _____ of Barbados.

c Guadaloupe is _____ of Martinique.

d Barbados is _____ of Grenada.

13 Use the scale on the map to estimate the distance between these places.

a Antigua and Barbuda: _____

b St Kitts and Nevis: _____

c Guadeloupe and Dominica: _____

d Grenada and Barbados: _____

14 Use the key on this map to find the names of one of these places.

a a church _____

b a historical site _____

c a beach _____

d an airport _____

e a hotel _____

Key

✈ Airport

⊕ Churches

Ⓗ Hotels

★ Historic Sites

☐ Major resort

15 Draw a map of your school's neighbourhood in the box. Make up a key to show the important places on the map.

Key:

16 Find these words in the puzzle.

BUILDING   LEGEND

CITIZEN   NATIONAL

DIRECTION   RESPECT

HERO   SCALE

HISTORY   SYMBOLS

Y	X	N	W	O	Z	B	I	V	S	T	A	Q	N	S
R	Q	L	E	X	R	Q	D	Y	P	T	P	O	N	C
O	W	T	T	Z	Q	E	M	Z	U	X	I	O	A	A
T	G	I	C	S	I	B	H	W	U	T	K	K	T	L
S	H	N	I	E	O	T	V	K	C	O	Q	Q	I	E
I	Y	I	I	L	P	T	I	E	I	V	W	O	O	Z
H	F	C	S	D	C	S	R	C	T	W	O	Q	N	N
I	T	M	A	Z	L	I	E	S	H	V	H	W	A	P
W	S	D	N	G	D	I	J	R	D	X	B	G	L	Y
N	P	R	S	N	Z	U	U	Y	D	N	E	G	E	L
G	P	P	S	J	G	C	H	B	W	G	M	W	X	A
B	V	F	P	X	X	M	S	D	U	I	Y	H	A	Z
G	W	A	Z	O	J	L	E	U	I	S	C	C	T	Y
H	D	S	V	I	B	I	G	O	E	U	P	O	J	W
S	O	L	K	Z	I	W	K	P	Z	Q	Z	E	L	S

4 How does a community work?

Student's Book pages 37–50

1 Look at the words in the box. Are they physical needs or social needs? Write them in the correct part of the table.

> love   shelter   help   clothes   feeling of belonging
>
> food   water   air

Physical needs	Social needs

2 Which of these are needs? Put a circle around each one.

3 Say why you think each of these needs is important.

a food

_____

_____

b clothing

_____

_____

c shelter

_____

_____

d water

_____

_____

e air

_____

_____

4 Make a list of some of the workers in your neighbourhood and say whether they provide goods or services.

Workers	Goods or services?

5 Match these tools to the workers who use them. Draw a line to link the worker and the tool.

Farmer   Fisherman   Carpenter   Firefighter   Doctor   Police officer

6 Use words from the box to fill in the blank spaces in the sentences.

autumn	buses	United States	seasons
football	fast	cold	winter	winter	spring
baseball	trains	apples	wheat	summer

a Some countries in the world are very different from Antigua and Barbuda,

like the _____ of America.

b It has four _____ .

c The seasons are _____, _____ ,

_____ and _____.

d In the summer people wear light clothes but in the _____

they have to wear very warm clothes.

e It gets very _____ in the winter.

f The main forms of public transport are _____ and

_____.

g They grow a lot of crops such as _____ and

_____ .

h The most popular sports are _____ and

_____ .

i They eat a lot of _____ food.

7 Draw a circle in one colour around the natural features, and a circle in another colour around the man-made features. You choose the colours, and show them in the key.

Key:

Natural feature

Man-made feature

Hill

House

Swamp

Forest

Cave

Bridge

Road

Beach

Lagoon

Dam

8 Give two reasons why a person may be unemployed.

_____

_____

_____

_____

_____

9 If a person is unemployed, what are some possible effects? Try to give three.

_____

_____

_____

_____

_____

10 What do you think might happen in a family if the parents become unemployed?

_____

_____

_____

_____

_____

_____

11 Find these words in the puzzle.

ACCEPTANCE

AIR

BELONGING

CLOTHING

FOOD

LOVE

NEEDS

OCCUPATION

PHYSICAL

SHELTER

SOCIAL

WANTS

L	F	F	N	I	A	L	I	B	R	V	A	O	B	P
L	A	K	G	O	G	P	H	Y	S	I	C	A	L	B
B	T	I	X	F	I	N	S	P	Q	Z	Z	S	Q	R
T	F	G	C	V	I	T	I	H	Q	B	S	T	A	X
I	U	I	M	O	L	E	A	G	E	G	X	N	D	P
R	Z	A	W	J	S	C	W	P	N	L	Z	A	G	N
V	C	F	B	D	I	N	I	O	U	O	T	W	K	Q
I	C	F	D	G	Z	A	R	U	W	C	L	E	W	E
I	E	L	H	C	C	T	O	I	Q	B	C	E	R	I
S	D	E	E	N	D	P	O	S	A	V	Z	O	B	T
W	L	R	F	O	G	E	C	L	O	T	H	I	N	G
Y	O	S	O	G	X	C	V	S	S	N	L	U	A	G
Q	V	F	M	H	H	C	Y	F	I	A	W	Q	T	W
C	E	R	R	D	H	A	M	L	L	V	V	P	S	D
R	C	N	X	W	Z	K	V	N	A	Q	M	A	T	D

5 Transportation

Student's Book pages 51–58

1 Use words from the box to fill in the blank spaces in the sentences.

air   transportation   cars   three   land

buses   water   bicycles

a Anything that is used to move people and goods from one place to another

is called _____ .

b People can move around the community by walking and by using

_____, _____ and _____.

c There are _____ main types of transportation.

d These are _____, _____ and

_____ .

2 The words in the box are all examples of transportation. Write them in the correct part of the table.

> bus   truck   ferry   train   bicycle   boat
>
> ship   yacht   airplane   van   car
>
> motorcycle   helicopter   cruise ship

Land	Water	Air

3 Read the sentences and for each one say which type of transportation would be best to use: land, sea or air.

a Shania and her mother wants to go from home to the supermarket.

_____

b Shania's mother ordered a car from Japan. How would it come to Antigua?

_____

c Shania and her family are going to New York for vacation.

_____

4 Write the names of four transportation centres in Antigua and Barbuda.

_____

_____

_____

_____

5 Draw lines to match each worker with the transportation centre that he or she works in.

6 Think about all the forms of transportation you have learned about.

a What form of transportation do you like most?

_____

b Which one would you like to try for the first time?

_____

7 Why are travel rules important?

_____

_____

_____

_____

8 What rules should you follow when using the school bus?

_____

_____

_____

_____

_____

_____

_____

9 Are these statements True or False? Write T or F after each one.

You should always:

a Walk in the middle of the road. ☐

b Walk facing the traffic coming towards you. ☐

c Cross the street when the traffic light is red for cars. ☐

d Use the pedestrian crossing. ☐

e Look left, not right, just before crossing the road. ☐

10 How can the government help in road safety?

_____

_____

_____

_____

_____

_____

_____

_____

_____

11 Draw a circle round three things done by the Transport Board.

Cut down trees   Mark roads   Provide traffic wardens

Issue drivers' licences   Build schools   Pick up garbage

12 There are good things and bad things about modern transportation. Some of them are listed below. Write the number of each one in the correct part of the table.

1. Cause air pollution

2. Cause traffic jams

3. Make travel easier

4. Make travel faster

5. Cause health problems

Good	Bad

13 Find these words in the puzzle.

AIR

HELICOPTER

LAND

OBEY

PEDESTRIAN

RULES

SAFETY

SEA

SIGNS

TRANSPORTATION

TRAVEL

WALK

L	A	N	D	J	U	L	U	M	X	Y	R	G	N	O
P	E	D	E	S	T	R	I	A	N	U	Q	O	I	M
W	A	L	K	O	K	T	K	U	L	A	I	Z	K	T
S	X	D	H	C	R	E	L	E	Z	T	J	H	W	U
Z	O	A	Q	N	B	N	S	M	A	H	I	S	J	Q
O	B	E	Y	W	I	B	K	T	E	M	X	G	D	P
G	K	F	B	W	R	Y	R	L	S	V	V	W	F	L
X	K	O	S	I	I	O	I	I	J	A	S	Y	U	U
V	I	Z	A	P	P	C	L	Q	U	H	F	E	H	I
E	Y	D	Q	S	O	T	R	A	V	E	L	E	A	T
U	B	B	N	P	K	J	Z	C	Z	A	C	A	T	S
E	Q	A	T	L	M	K	W	I	I	K	M	B	P	Y
H	R	E	S	I	G	N	S	V	F	Y	H	C	T	Q
T	R	N	V	P	I	A	S	E	A	B	Q	M	Y	V
W	I	E	F	P	P	F	W	T	D	U	N	X	S	E

6 Looking after our community

Student's Book pages 59–66

1 Use words from the box to fill in the blank spaces in the sentences. Some words may be used more than once.

> environment   needs   resources   water
>
> natural   man-made   chair   survive

a Natural _____ are things we find in the

_____ around us.

b We use resources to help us _____.

c There are two types of resources. These are _____

and _____.

d _____ resources are things like buildings and

a _____.

e Natural resources are things like soil and _____.

2 Look at these pictures of natural resources. Write what each one is below the picture.

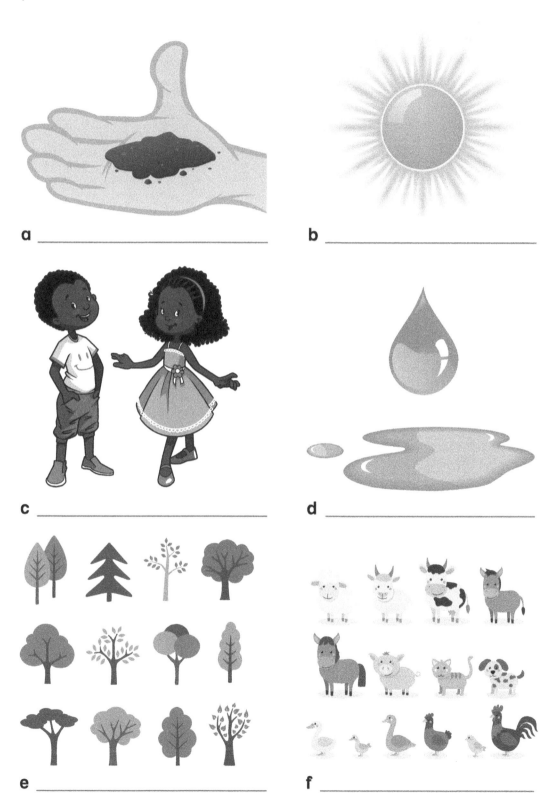

a _____

b _____

c _____

d _____

e _____

f _____

3 Think of six man-made resources. Find or draw a picture of each one. Write the name of each one underneath it.

1.

2.

3.

4.

5.

6.

4 Find pictures of four trees and plants found in your community. Stick each one in one of the boxes and then write its name below. They should be different from the trees and plants shown in the Student's Book.

5 How are trees used?

a How are trees used by people?

_____

_____

_____

b How are trees used by animals?

_____

_____

_____

6 What do you think would happen to us if there were no plants or trees?

_____

_____

_____

_____

_____

7 Give two uses for each of these natural resources.

a land

_____

_____

b water

_____

_____

c animals

_____

_____

8 Colour this in. You can use the colours in the Student's Book or you can choose your own.

9 Fill in the diagram to show four ways we can conserve our resources.

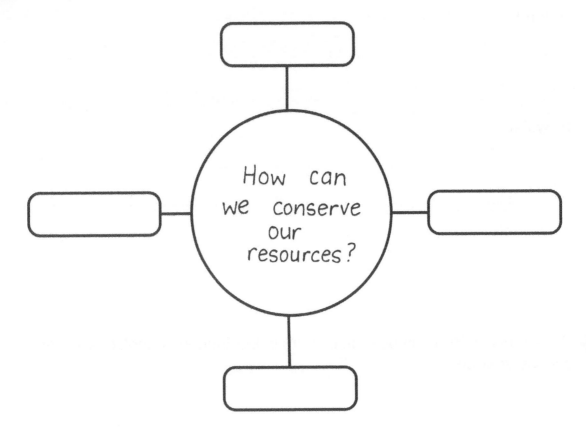

10 Use words from the box to fill in the blank spaces in the sentences about pollution.

> garbage   pollution   clean   litter

a When we make the land dirty it is called _____ .

b We need to keep the land _____

c We should not _____.

d We should always throw our _____ into a covered bin.

11 Use words from the box to fill in the blank spaces in the sentences about the weather.

> **windy**   **rainy**   **quickly**   **sunny**   **cloudy**   **weather**

a The _____ is things like wind, sun and rain.

b It can change very _____.

c We use words like _____, _____,

_____ and _____ to describe the weather.

12 Write the type of weather shown in each picture.

a _____

b _____

c _____

d _____

59

13 How does the weather affect our natural resources?

14 Find the words below in the puzzle.

ANIMALS

CLEAN

CONSERVE

MANMADE

NATURAL

PEOPLE

POLLUTION

RESOURCES

SOIL

USEFUL

WATER

WEATHER

S	N	I	O	J	S	V	O	E	L	U	F	E	S	U
E	P	O	B	R	W	X	V	W	S	B	W	Z	Z	B
C	E	X	I	X	E	R	P	C	A	O	Z	C	B	A
R	O	N	L	T	E	N	R	X	Y	T	I	B	V	J
U	P	E	A	S	U	W	H	N	M	X	P	L	T	T
O	L	R	N	T	C	L	P	T	U	Q	R	W	S	I
S	E	O	A	U	U	L	L	M	A	N	M	A	D	E
E	C	K	N	S	V	R	E	O	C	F	F	R	P	R
R	E	W	I	B	U	S	A	A	P	R	E	T	A	W
X	F	O	M	U	Q	H	S	L	N	M	T	R	K	C
A	V	P	A	Z	H	M	H	D	I	E	F	L	G	Y
S	Z	U	L	D	W	M	M	U	Z	H	D	Z	A	I
R	Q	S	S	P	A	H	P	O	P	N	K	B	P	F
S	L	W	I	W	E	A	T	H	E	R	U	V	X	Z
X	Q	D	J	N	O	L	O	A	M	W	V	N	Y	S

7 Communicating

Student's Book pages 67–72

1 Use words from the box to fill in the blank spaces in the sentences.

> **non-verbal** **communication** **verbal** **important**
>
> **feel** **understand**

a The passing of ideas and information from one person to the next

is called _____.

b Communication is very _____.

c We use it to show how we _____ and to

_____ what others are saying to us.

d There are two main types of communication: _____ and

_____ .

2 Fill in the missing words in the diagram to show what is needed for communication to take place.

3 Verbal or non-verbal? Read the sentences and say if the communication used is verbal or non–verbal in each one.

a John waved his hand to Sarah. _____

b They drew pictures of their favourite toys. _____

c John's mother called him on the phone. _____

d He frowned when he hung up the phone. _____

e He told Sarah he had to go home. _____

4 List three communication centres in Antigua and Barbuda and say how each one is used.

a _____

_____

_____

b _____

_____

_____

c _____

_____

_____

5 Write a list of eight ways that we communicate.

_____

_____

_____

_____

_____

_____

_____

_____

6 How would the messages below probably be sent? Choose from the box.

| email | phone | radio | newspaper |

a High winds are expected later today.   _____

b I would like to invite you to my birthday party.   _____

c There is a story about the missing twins
on page 3.   _____

d Shania's mom needs to come home right
away from her vacation.   _____

7 List three things you should do, to communicate clearly and politely.

_____

_____

_____

_____

_____

_____

8 Look at these ways of communicating. Some of them were done long ago and some are only done now. Write them in the correct part of the table. Be careful! Some can go in both columns.

Letter **Fire** **Radio** **Telephone** **Email**

Talking **Notice board** **Social media** **Drums**

Long ago	Today

9 Say how we would probably use each of the following social media apps to communicate.

a Facebook

_____

_____

b WhatsApp

_____

_____

c Instagram

_____

_____

d Snapchat

_____

_____

10 Find these words in the puzzle.

COMMUNICATION

EMAIL

FACEBOOK

GESTURES

LETTERS

MESSAGE

MOBILE

VERBAL

RECEIVER

SENDER

SIGNS

SYMBOLS

TELEPHONE

NON-VERBAL

N	J	I	Y	S	M	S	P	O	L	N	E	O	R	V
O	O	S	P	I	R	M	R	A	K	S	Z	E	O	X
F	V	I	H	C	M	E	B	P	L	P	C	P	S	E
B	C	G	T	O	I	R	T	F	J	E	Y	A	Q	L
V	X	O	H	A	E	S	L	T	I	M	X	E	G	I
C	G	X	B	V	C	W	L	V	E	K	Z	F	E	B
M	X	C	N	N	W	I	E	O	X	L	P	Q	N	O
T	U	O	M	M	W	R	N	S	B	T	I	D	O	M
P	N	E	M	A	I	L	E	U	I	M	O	S	H	R
S	E	R	U	T	S	E	G	G	M	G	Y	H	P	Y
F	A	C	E	B	O	O	K	S	A	M	N	S	E	O
R	E	D	N	E	S	A	R	W	E	S	O	S	L	I
N	C	M	X	Y	V	E	R	B	A	L	S	C	E	C
B	H	E	A	O	N	X	C	X	C	P	W	E	T	G
C	O	M	C	V	B	G	G	E	R	M	P	D	M	Y

Notes

Notes

Notes

Notes

Notes